A RAGE IN HARLEM :

JUNE JORDAN AND ARCHITECTURE

by **NIKIL SAVAL**

————October 29, 2020
Open House Lecture
Gund Hall Virtual Event
Harvard University
Graduate School of Design

————Introduced by Sarah M. Whiting————
Produced by Ken Stewart, Paige K. Johnston, and Kat Chavez
———— Published by the Harvard University Graduate School
of Design and Sternberg Press

Note from the Speaker

My account of the Harlem rebellion is largely drawn from Michael W. Flamm, *In the Heat of the Summer: The New York Riots of 1964 and the War on Crime* (Philadelphia: University of Pennsylvania Press, 2016).

SARAH M. WHITING: Welcome to the Harvard GSD Fall 2020 Open House Lecture. —— I'm delighted to welcome writer, editor, community organizer, and candidate Nikil Saval. If you're registered to vote in the state of Pennsylvania, please note that Nikil is the Democratic nominee for the first senate district of Pennsylvania, which extends from Rittenhouse Square to South Philadelphia. —— As a nonprofit organization, the GSD is prohibited from endorsing candidates or from being partisan. So let me leave it at this: Everyone who is eligible to vote on Tuesday, November 3, should please do so. Nothing is more important than exercising that right, and adding your voice to the furthering of our democracy.

I'm very grateful to the GSD's Trevor O'Brien, and to the Election Day volunteers, who've made it possible to maintain Gund Hall as a safe polling place despite the pandemic. And I encourage everyone to walk, cycle, or drive by Gund after dark, starting tomorrow evening, to see the fabulous work of our communications and exhibitions team: an animation on the Cambridge Street facade of Gund, designed by Chad Kloepfer and installed by Dan Borelli and David Zimmerman-Stuart, encouraging voting. Chad's bold, succinct, and positive "Go vote!" animation does a lot to counter the hyperpolarized, divisive, and disrespectful rhetoric and behavior that's featuring new lows in public debates, in public spaces, and on social media. —————— During this turbulent time, I encourage each one of us to pause and reaffirm the GSD's core values: respecting the rights, differences, and dignity of others, and treating all people with decency and respect. It's our mission to advance design as well as critical inquiry, all the while remaining focused on attacking issues rather than people.

And that brings me back to Nikil Saval. Nikil models exactly the kind of discourse that helps to advance the world rather than bring it to an acrimonious standstill. His writing and activism relate to every one of our disciplines and programs. ———He was previously coeditor and now remains a board member of the politically engaged literary magazine *n+1*. He's also a contributing writer for the *New Yorker* and the *New York Times*, covering architecture, urbanism, and design. You might have spotted his recent article, "Design for the Future When the Future is Bleak," from a few Sundays ago. Additionally, Nikil cofounded the activist organization Reclaim Philadelphia, which fights for a world without structural racism, classism, sexism, and oppression by advocating for health care, education, a livable environment, housing, safety, and justice as human rights.

Tonight, Nikil is going to combine his writing self and his political self, and his activist hat and his urban historian hat, to take us back to a difficult moment in 1964 that has direct resonance with today, and to the collaborative, radical reconstruction and speculation that that moment inspired. ———— I'm absolutely thrilled, Nikil, that you're committing precious time out of your campaign schedule to spend this evening with us, to share this important example. I look forward to your talk, and to the conversation afterward. ———— Nikil welcomes questions about his talk, his writing more broadly, his campaign, or whatever else strikes your fancy. ———— Thank you, and welcome to the GSD, Nikil.

THE INCIDENTS

THE INCIDENTS

NIKIL SAVAL: Thank you so much, Dean Whiting. Thank you to the GSD for inviting me to speak. And thank you to Paige, Kat, Matthew for all your technical assistance, and to Ken Stewart for all the work that you've offered. I know arranging these talks is very time-consuming and difficult, and I appreciate all your guidance. Thank you, all the students attending. I know this must be a very strange year, especially if this is your first year. And thank you to everyone else tuning in, to everyone taking time to hear this. —————— I'm excited to speak about a moment in 1964, and specifically the work of June Jordan, who is often known as a poet, writer, and novelist, but who I'm treating here as something that I believe that she was: a designer and architect. Just to give a content warning, I will discuss police brutality and I will discuss racism and racism from police, as well as allude to racist language and racial slurs, without necessarily using them myself. I just want people to be aware this is coming. —————— So, with that, I'll start this lecture on June Jordan. Here we go.

Lieutenant Kills Negro Youth; 300 Teen-Agers Harass Police

Continued From Page 1, Col. 2

Coyle of the Manhattan North Detectives.

"The youths and the superintendent had some heated words," Inspector Coyle said, "and then the superintendent ran into the building with the boys in pursuit."

Lieutenant Gilligan, according to the police official, was in a television repair shop next to the apartment house. He had taken a small radio there for repairs, and on hearing the commotion, left the store to investigate.

"The officer was dressed in civilian clothes," Inspector Coyle said. "He saw the boys banging on an apartment door with a garbage can lid and ordered them to stop."

"He showed his shield and one of the boys [later identified as Powell] came after him with a knife. Powell refused to heed the lieutenant's instructions and continued toward him with the knife in his hand. The lieutenant warned him but the youth raised the knife."

The police official said that Lieutenant Gilligan then drew his service revolver and warned

Lieut. Thomas Gilligan of 14th Division in Brooklyn.

shouting at the policemen. Bot-

[*Slide*] A Rage in Harlem: June Jordan and Architecture.
———— On June 2, 1964, President Lyndon B. Johnson signed the Civil Rights Act into law. ———— [*Slide*] Two weeks later, on Thursday, July 16, James Gilligan, an off-duty police officer in New York, shot and killed a 15-year-old Black high school student, James Powell. At the time, Powell was attending summer school on the east side of Manhattan for voluntary remedial reading classes at a junior high school. He was thought of poorly by neighbors, who expressed barely veiled racial prejudice toward him and toward his fellow high school classmates, most of them Black, as they loitered waiting for classes to start every morning. ———— So too was he thought of poorly by the criminal justice system. He had been caught many times by police for minor transgressions, like trying to board subways and buses without paying the fare. The morning of July 16, Patrick Lynch, a white superintendent for a building housing white tenants, was washing his sidewalk with a hose. He apparently repeatedly asked a group of students to move from the sidewalk so that he could water flowers and a fire escape above their heads. When they did not, he apparently, according to the students and another eyewitness, sprayed them with water and called them "dirty n-words," and said that he was going to "wash the Black off you."———— The students responded by throwing bottles, trash, and trash can lids at Lynch, who ran inside the building. Powell ran up the steps of the building, supposedly screaming, "hit him, hit him, hit him." Officer Gilligan was inside the Jadco TV Service Company across the street. He rushed out the store, taking out his badge and his revolver.

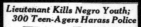

Lieutenant Kills Negro Youth; 300 Teen-Agers Harass Police

Continued From Page 1, Col. 2

Coyle of the Manhattan North Detectives.

"The youths and the superintendent had some heated words," Inspector Coyle said, "and then the superintendent ran into the building with the boys in pursuit."

Lieutenant Gilligan, according to the police official, was in a television repair shop next to the apartment house. He had taken a small radio there for repairs, and on hearing the commotion, left the store to investigate.

"The officer was dressed in civilian clothes," Inspector Coyle said. "He saw the boys banging on an apartment door with a garbage can lid and ordered them to stop."

"He showed his shield and one of the boys [later identified as Powell] came after him with a knife. Powell refused to heed the lieutenant's instructions and continued toward him with the knife in his hand. The lieutenant warned him but the youth raised the knife."

The police official said that Lieutenant Gilligan then drew his service revolver and warned

Lieut. Thomas Gilligan of 14th Division in Brooklyn.

shouting at the policemen. Bot-

What happened next is disputed. According to the adult witnesses, most of whom were white, this is what happened. Powell, who was returning down the stairs, tried to strike Gilligan while holding a knife in his right hand. Gilligan fired his gun. Powell tried to stab Gilligan with his knife, but Gilligan blocked and pushed him. But Powell had managed to slice Gilligan's arm in the process. And when he raised his hand again, Gilligan fired his gun. ———— The shot rebounded off Powell's wrist into his chest. As Powell continued forward, Gilligan stepped back, and fired again into Powell's abdomen. He fell on the sidewalk, face down. Powell's friend ran over and asked the officer to call an ambulance. "No," he said. "This Black [*expletive*] is my prisoner," Gilligan replied, according to Powell's friend. "You call an ambulance." By the time the ambulance arrived, Powell was dead. ———— Most of the 15 Black students who were witnesses saw the confrontation differently. They said that Powell was unarmed and unthreatening. "I saw the boy go into the building," one teenage girl reported, "and he didn't have any knife then. When he came out, he was even laughing, and kind of like running. And the cop was on the street going into the building. And then he shot him."———— It was well known in Harlem that most police officers had throwaway knives on them, because they would suffer disciplinary charges for the unwarranted use of force. Whether or not Powell had a knife on him in this case—and there was one found several feet away from the scene—there were numerous well-known cases in Harlem where people were killed by police officers then, as there are numerous cases today, despite being unthreatening and unarmed. They also said that Gilligan did not identify himself as a police officer.

THE INCIDENTS

[*Slide*] An immediate chain of events was set into motion, though every part of it was contingent and unexpected in its progression. Students began converging on the scene. One hundred police officers arrived in riot gear, taking three women into custody, then eventually releasing them. Fifty students attacked a newsstand at 77th Street, not far from the offices of the Congress of Racial Equality, or CORE. Demonstrations continued peacefully the next day. The evening of Saturday, July 18, around 150 people followed a pastor from Fountain Spring Baptist Church to the police station in the heart of Harlem. The crowd grew to 250, and chanted, "murder, murder." And they sang, referring to police commissioner Michael Murphy, "Murphy is a bastard, he must be removed. Murphy is a bastard, he must be removed."—singing to the tune of "We Shall Not Be Moved." A confrontation developed, eventually overtaking much of central Harlem. By Sunday morning, one person was dead, 31 were injured, and 30 arrested. The entrance to Harlem Hospital was spattered with blood.

THE INCIDENTS

[*Slide*] At the time, June Jordan was living in housing projects across the Queensboro Bridge in Brooklyn. She just completed work on a film, *The Cool World*, produced by Frederick Wiseman and directed by Shirley Clarke, that took place in Harlem with a nearly all-Black cast of non-professional actors. She was embarking on a freelance writing career. Her first commissioned piece was for the *New York Herald Tribune* about the Freedom National Bank, a Black-owned institution meant to serve Black people in Harlem. ——— Asked by her editor to figure out whether the summer of 1964 would be "a long hot summer," she concluded, "it should be one." Her editor, Jordan reported, declined to accept her conclusions, and wanted to argue with her after he returned from covering the Republican convention in California, where Barry Goldwater was to accept the party's nomination for President.

THE INCIDENTS

[*Slide*] At the convention, former President Eisenhower depart-
ed from his prepared remarks and warned about the danger
posed by urban crime. "Let us not be guilty," Eisenhower said,
"of maudlin sympathy for the criminal who, roaming the
streets with a switchblade knife and illegal firearms seeking a
helpless prey, suddenly becomes upon apprehension a poor,
underprivileged person who counts upon the compassion of
our society and the laxness or weaknesses of too many courts
to forgive his offense."———— Riots and rebellions became
a theme of the Republican convention: a way of uniting con-
cerns of Republicans in the North, as well as Dixiecrats leaving
the Democratic party to become Republicans in the South,
while this question of urban crime was becoming a live question in New York City and Harlem.

THE INCIDENTS

[*Slide*] Jordan heard about the Saturday night riot the next day on the radio. She said, "Newscasters seemingly competed in hysterical warnings and reports of official pleas to the Harlem community not to duplicate the preceding night's terror. I disbelieved, as a matter of principle, the hysteria and took off on my hour's walk to find a newspaper."——— She found news that James Powell's funeral services would take place that night. "I had been shocked and enraged to read two or three days earlier," she wrote, "of the murder of this boy, half the size of the big Irish cop wearing no uniform and elect- ing to shoot a kid who allegedly held a penknife. This cop, Gilligan, is the recipient of a citation for four times disarming men. I decided to pay my respects to the boy."——— Entering Harlem from the Triborough Bridge, Jordan said she found "a challenge to credulity. Literally scores and scores of helmeted, white policemen patrolled the streets in hubs of 25 or 30 each. There were more policemen than people on any main street. The presence of so many policemen began to make me ner- vous, frightened, and angry. We went to the 38th parallel," as she described it, "132nd Street and 7th Avenue. Past this cor- ner, no one was allowed. Buses began to arrive, taxis, civilian automobiles, fire engines with sadistic screeching—all vehicles jammed with policemen. The territory was clearly invaded. I could not believe it when still another bus would brake to a stop at that intersection and disgorge still another hundred combatants. Overhead, helicopters dawdled and dived and contributed to the unreal scene of a full-scale war with no one but enemies in view. Bottles began to pelt the street, aiming at police cars, policemen," she wrote.

THE INCIDENTS

[*Slide*] "Every time there was a hit, the probably thousand of us on both sides of the street would yell and applaud. Cops were firing endlessly now. They would stand on the curb and fire up at all the windows of the tenement buildings. People were screaming obscenities: MOTHER FUCKERS SHITS WHITE SHITS WHITE MOTHER FUCKERS BASTARDS MURDERERS GILLIGAN GILLIGAN." Jordan moved between the streets and makeshift clinics and Harlem Hospital.
——— [*Slide*] "My main accomplishment that night," she wrote, "was not to vomit. I had never seen the back of a bashed-in head, a kneecap split by a bullet—blood….People sat on waiting benches, blood pouring from wherever they'd been hit….We all felt completely defeated. Only the endless harassment of danger, of really running from the guns, kept all of us awake and going….Every seventh word in the Harlem crowds, by the way, was *GOLDWATER*. My sentiments exactly."

THE INCIDENTS

[*Slide*] A week after the riot, Jordan's husband wrote to her saying that he was not returning home from his graduate studies in anthropology in Chicago. Jordan was effectively separated, and she was now forced to raise her son Christopher alone. After another week, *Esquire* magazine proposed that Jordan write a piece.

3 Letter to R. Buckminster Fuller (1964)

A week after the riot, my husband wrote, saying he was not coming back.

Another week went by. *Esquire* asked me to write for them. I proposed a collaboration with Bucky Fuller; he was the only person I was willing to try; maybe working with him could save me from the hatred I felt, and the complete misery I felt, the want.

When it became firm that Bucky and I would collaborate on an architectural redesign of Harlem, I put my whole life on the line: Now I would work and work and work and wait on this beginning, as a writer, thinker, poet.

There was no money. The advance, gallantly extracted from *Esquire* by Bucky, went quickly. Christopher could not come back to me from his grandparents because I had no money to support him. Michael was gone. I worked. I studied architecture. I wrote to Bucky. I planned. I spent my life waiting. It was a gamble.

Those days I didn't eat. A few friends brought me cigarettes, Scotch, eggs, bread, and my mother gave me two or three dollars for gas money. What I had left was my car: my tangible liberty was my car. I lived like this until *Esquire* said, okay, you're done: It will be published. That was seven months away.

That December, Bucky came to town. We met. I showed him my final draft. He approved it. We walked over to *Esquire*. They approved it. They said they'd send me the money. It came: December 24, 1964. Christopher came back: December

23

[*Slide*] She responded by suggesting a collaboration with R. Buckminster Fuller, the then unclassifiable—and still unclassifiable—thinker and designer who considered himself a "philosopher of shelter."———"[H]e was the only person I was willing to try," Jordan wrote. "[M]aybe working with him could save me from the hatred I felt, and the complete misery I felt, the want. When it became firm that Bucky and I would collaborate on an architectural redesign of Harlem, I put my whole life on the line: Now I would work and work and work and wait on this beginning, as a writer, thinker, poet."

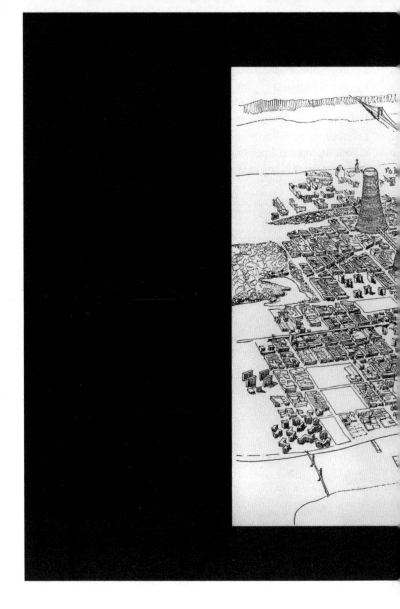

THE INCIDENTS

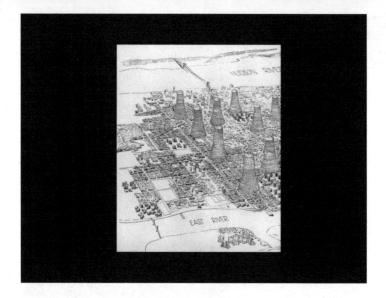

THE INCIDENTS

[*Slide*] The project that came out of it is "Skyrise for Harlem," and here we see an image of the *Esquire* spread. The editors re-titled it "Instant Slum Clearance," but in my talk I refer to it by Jordan's original title, "Skyrise for Harlem."——"Skyrise for Harlem" is an unprecedented and unequaled collaboration between a white designer who uneasily flits in and out of architectural history, and a Black designer who is virtually never considered part of that history. It is a creative response to the despair and negativity that is itself a form of annihilation. It was a complete redesign of a dense urban neighborhood, one of the most symbolic and actually fraught areas in the United States. Moreover, it was a response to an urban rebellion that took physical architectural form when all of the words bound up in the project—*Harlem*, *housing*, *architecture*— were perhaps at the peak of their contestation. It was also an attempt to provide a social solution to what was largely thought of by many people as a community at once sublimely disinvested in and self-consuming through violence. It was a distinct kind of project within a recognizably abolitionist framework. While the response to police brutality and mass incarceration is often captured by the idea of taking resources from one institution, from police and prisons, and giving it to another—from *defunding*, say, the police—here was a proposal that was generative and took form in space. —— Though this multiple-tower housing proposal for Harlem they designed together never came to fruition, it represented one in a series of moments in which Black artistic figures working with architects, or people on the edge of architecture, began to take hold of urban space in an attempt to develop housing.

THE INCIDENTS

[*Slide*] Some years later, Amiri Baraka, the poet, playwright, and organizer working in Newark, broke ground on a Black nationalist–inspired, low-income housing project funded by the New Jersey Housing Finance Authority, known as the Kawaida Towers. This effort we don't often talk about is also connected to the effort we do frequently recognize—and I say "we" here as students of architectural history and urban history—and the one to which more obviously we are the heirs: the attempt to transform the design of housing and urban space to prevent crime. While Jordan, Baraka, and others tried to construct and own new forms of housing, white designers and white critics of urban renewal programs proposed the demolition of existing public housing, and its replacement by lower-density housing that would ultimately reduce the number of actual public housing units and focus so much of its efforts on crime prevention. ——— This lineage descends, I argue, from Jane Jacobs, and runs straight to right-wing administrations in the United States, and also the United Kingdom, which sought an end to public housing and attempted to dismantle it. All of this requires looking back on Jane Jacobs's canonical *Death and Life of Great American Cities*, less as an attack on current vogues and city planning as it was described, and more as a manual on crime prevention. In both cases we are talking about today—both histories—design was elevated as having a potentially palliative, or uplifting, impact on society, and an outsized influence on public behavior.

THE INCIDENTS

[*Slide*] Before attending to the details of "Skyrise for Harlem," its genesis as a project, and its impact and afterlife, I want to take into account the material and discursive context in which it emerged. For one thing, there was the fact that "Skyrise" expressed a bifurcated Harlem, one that acknowledged Harlem's history and future as a Black neighborhood, even as *the* Black neighborhood, while even sympathetic writers and thinkers worried over it. Well into the 1960s, it retained an idea of itself as a Black capital, with Malcolm X operating from Harlem and Fidel Castro visiting him in 1960. ———— But at the same time, urban rebellions and displacement were felt to sap at the life of the neighborhood. "Harlem," begins Jordan's article for *Esquire*, "is life dying inside a closet, an excrescence beginning where a green park ends, a self-perpetuating disintegration of walls, ceilings, doorways, lives."

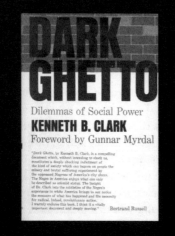

THE INCIDENTS

[*Slide*] The urban historian Daniel Matlin has noted that her language is "suffused with the liberal pathologist imagery of Black urban life that had intensified since the 1940s and now peaked in 1965"—the same year that saw the publication of Kenneth B. Clark's psychological study, *Dark Ghetto*, and Claude Brown's memoir, *Manchild in the Promised Land*, both of which were about Harlem's degeneration, as well as the leaking of the federal government's 1965 Moynihan Report on the "crumbling Black family." Chester Himes, the noir novelist whose novel, *The Rage in Harlem*—that's where I take my title—described Harlem as "an American cancer."——— Jordan also pointed out in her article that half of Harlem's children live with one parent or none, echoing the obsession with Black family structures. At times, this took on a prophetic or even an apocalyptic tempo. "Walk through the streets and see what we, this nation, have become," James Baldwin wrote of Harlem in 1960.

THE INCIDENTS

[*Slide*] At the same time urban renewal projects divided and overwhelmed the area. As historian Brian Goldstein writes in his article, "The Search for New Forms: Black Power and the Making of the Postmodern City": "Harlem was by no means the only New York City community transformed by the urban renewal of the 1950s and 1960s, but it represented a favored site for officials seeking ambitious redevelopment of the built environment."———— Three public housing complexes were erected in central Harlem in the '50s and '60s: the Polo Grounds Houses, Colonial Park Houses, and St. Nicholas Houses; as well as two middle-income housing developments that transformed 24 acres on Lenox Avenue. In East Harlem, New York City spent $250 million to build several projects that would house 62,400 residents. One project, the James Weldon Johnson Houses, which is seen being built in this image here, took up six city blocks. ———— By the 1960s there was a growing sense among residents and critics alike that the project of renewal had failed. Jordan in her writing refers to the quote, "Urban renewal means Negro removal." James Baldwin called Harlem's public housing "colorless, bleak, high, and revolting." And he proposed the existence of a law, apparently respected throughout the world, that public housing shall be as "cheerless as a prison."

THE INCIDENTS

[*Slide*] In the conventional understanding of an architect as a licensed practitioner, Jordan was not one. But in the understanding of someone who sought to propose and build interventions in public space, she was. ——— Her interest in architecture was partly the result of academic training—she had studied it somewhat at Barnard College—and autodidacticism. "Architecture became an obsession," she writes in her book, *Civil Wars*, "that I satisfied by, once a week, going into Manhattan on the night the Donnell library," pictured here, "stayed open late, to browse among the architectural journals and textbooks in the downstairs art reading room. [*Slide*] This was my one evening out, every week: Michael," her husband, "would come home by 6 o'clock, if humanly possible, and I would then leave him and Christopher," her son, "to eat the dinner I had already prepared, and rush to the corner bus stop."

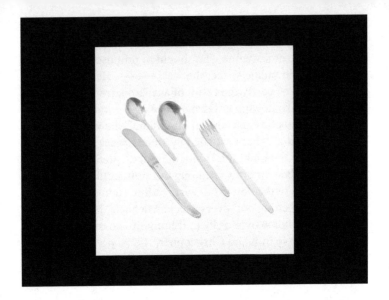

THE INCIDENTS

"At the Donnell, I lost myself among rooms and doorways and Japanese gardens and Bauhaus chairs and spoons. The picture of a spoon, of an elegant, spare utensil as common in its purpose as a spoon, and as lovely and singular in its form as sculpture, utterly transformed my ideas about the possibilities of design in relation to human existence. [*Slide*] If my mother had held such a spoon, if I could have given her such a useful piece of beauty even once, perhaps everything would have been different for her: she who committed suicide not so many years later: she who admired but never wore the dress-up overcoat that my cousin and father gave to her, and which she 'saved' in the closet, until her death. If I could make things as simple, as necessary, and as wonderful as a spoon of Bauhaus design, then I could be sure, in a deep way, of doing some good, of changing, for instance, the kitchen where I grew up, baffled by the archaeological layers of aimless, wrong-year calendars, and high-gloss clashing wall colors, and four cans of paprika and endlessly dysfunctional clutter and material of no morale, of clear degenerating morass and mire, of slum, of resignation."——— I just want to point out, this spoon is by Wilhelm Wagenfeld. It is not a Bauhaus design. Just clarifying, for the architecture students. You probably already recognize that.

THE INCIDENTS

[*Slide*] It was in the Donnell that Jordan first came across the work of Buckminster Fuller. "Photographs of his inventions," she writes, "led me into a biography and then into his own writings: *Nine Chains to the Moon, Education Automation*, and so on. Even more than Corbusier," she wrote, "Fuller's thinking weighed upon my own as a hunch yet to be gambled on the American landscape, where, daily, deathly polarization of peoples according to skin gained in horror as white violence escalated against Black life."——— The spirit of revelation that seizes June Jordan in the Donnell library, confronting the Bauhaus spoon, and imagining her mother's life taking a different turn, has its analog in Buckminster Fuller's mythologizing of his own life. He told often of how, in 1927, he was walking out through the north side of Chicago and sat by the waters of Lake Michigan. He was 32, jobless, penniless, nearly homeless, a failure. It was winter, and he calculated how long it would take him to freeze to death in the icy waters. As he readied himself for the plunge, he found all of a sudden that he could not. He was, in fact, no longer on the ground. He was being lifted, he was floating, and he was being spoken to. Whether the voice was coming from inside or outside his head, he couldn't quite tell. ———"You do not have the right to eliminate yourself," the voice told him. "You do not belong to you. You belong to the universe." His mind was there to be shared with the world: such was Fuller's calling. And so, he went home. He told his wife that he did not need a job. He told his wife that his job now was simply to think. He spent the next two years in rapt silence, filling five thousand pages of notebooks with drawings, ideas, plans. He felt he had the salvation of humanity in his grasp.

THE INCIDENTS

[*Slide*] That salvation combined a number of different trends: the design of low-cost shelter, with the efficiency to house millions; many people also recognize this tetrahedron or geodesic dome shape that he was obsessed with, from his idea of tensile integrity structures. ———— As the journalist Douglas Murphy notes in his book *Last Futures*, a study of utopian architecture of the 1970s, Fuller was an early advocate of moving away from a carbon-based energy system, arguing, "the energy that had gone into making coal and oil over millions of years would be drastically wasted if it were to be completely depleted in just a few hundred years." He was a utopian by necessity: humanity would simply not survive if it did not adapt and work out systems of efficient construction, of basic fundamental shelter that would allow it to survive. ————"This generation," he said, "knows that man can do anything he wants, you see. These people know that wealth is not money—that it's a combination of physical energy and human intellect—and they know that energy can be neither created nor destroyed and that intellectual knowledge can only increase, and that therefore total wealth cannot help but increase. They also know that they can generate far more wealth by cooperation on a global scale than by competition with each other. And they realize—or at least they sense—that utopia is possible now, for the first time in history." Still, in the same breath he also doubted it: "I think it is absolutely touch-and-go whether we are going to make it."

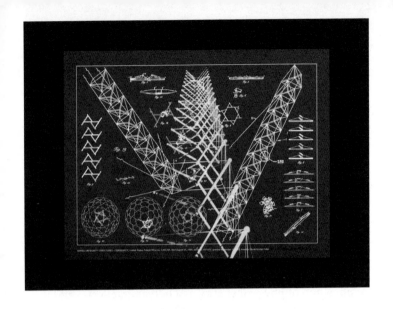

THE INCIDENTS

Reflecting on her reaction to the Harlem Riot of 1964, as she termed it, Jordan wrote that the week afterward was "a week of lurching around downtown streets like a war-zone refugee (whenever I heard a police or fire engine siren I would literally hit the pavement to flatten myself before the putative level of the flying bullets) that I realized I was now filled with hatred for everything and everyone white. Almost simultaneously it came to me that this condition, if it lasted, would mean that I had lost the point: not to resemble my enemies, not to dwarf my world, not to lose my willingness and ability to love."———
"So," she continued, "back in 1964, I resolved not to run on hatred but instead to use what I loved, words, for the sake of the people I loved. However, beyond my people, I did not know the content of my love: what was *I* for? Nevertheless, the agony of that moment propelled me into a reaching far and away to R. Buckminster Fuller, to whom I proposed a collaborative architectural redesign of Harlem, as my initial, deliberated movement away from the hateful, the divisive."

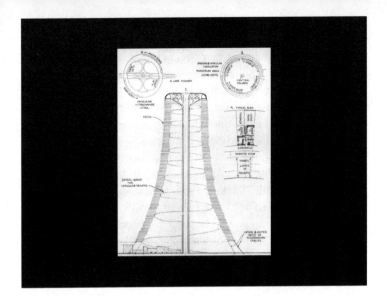

THE INCIDENTS

[*Slide*] "My first meeting with Bucky lasted several hours," she writes, "just the two of us, alone," in Fuller's room at the St. Regis Hotel. "And when we separated, agreed on the collaboration for *Esquire* magazine, I felt safe in my love again. We would think and work together to design a three-dimensional, enviable, exemplary life situation for Harlem residents who, otherwise, had to outmaneuver New York City's Tactical Police Force, rats, a destructive and compulsory system of education, and so forth, or die."———— Jordan's early descriptions to Fuller started with conditions and needs. Her conditions were that keeping warm is a matter of locating the absentee landlord in Harlem, rather than an independent expedition to gather wood for a fire. And the needs she identified: "I would think," she wrote, "that this new reality of Harlem should immediately reassure its residents that control of the quality of survival is possible and that every life is valuable."————"Following the Harlem Riot of 1964," she wrote in her article, "a profusion of remedies for what was at last accepted as a critical situation appeared everywhere; nowhere, however, was environmental redesign given prime emphasis. Yet it is architecture, conceived of in its fullest meaning as the creation of environment, which may actually determine the pace, pattern, and quality of living experience."———— When published in *Esquire* in 1965, as I noted before, the editors changed the title from "Skyrise for Harlem" to "Instant Slum Clearance." Though she was by then divorced, June Jordan was referred to by her married name, June Meyer. And any contribution she had made to the project was edited out. The design was referred to as exclusively belonging to Fuller. These series of erasures of individuals, communities, neighborhoods, titles were both the opposite of what Jordan intended, and partly of a piece with the article.

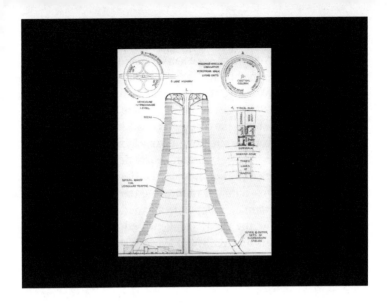

THE INCIDENTS

[*Slide*] Here's an image of the design. It's a poor image, but we'll get to another one later. ———— To quote the article's first paragraph again: "Harlem is a life dying inside a closet, an excrescence beginning where a green park ends, a self-perpetuating disintegration of walls, ceilings, doorways, lives...Redevelopment generally means the removal of slum residents while land is cleared for new building and new purposes. In fact, 'redevelopment' is frequently a pretext for the permanent expulsion of Negro populations. Fuller's design permits all residents to remain on site while new and vastly improved dwelling facilities rise directly over the old. No one will move anywhere but up."

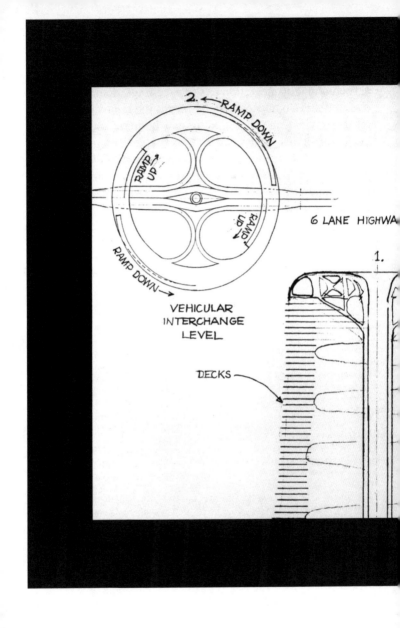

2. ← RAMP DOWN

RAMP UP →

RAMP UP →

RAMP DOWN →

6 LANE HIGHWAY

1.

VEHICULAR
INTERCHANGE
LEVEL

DECKS

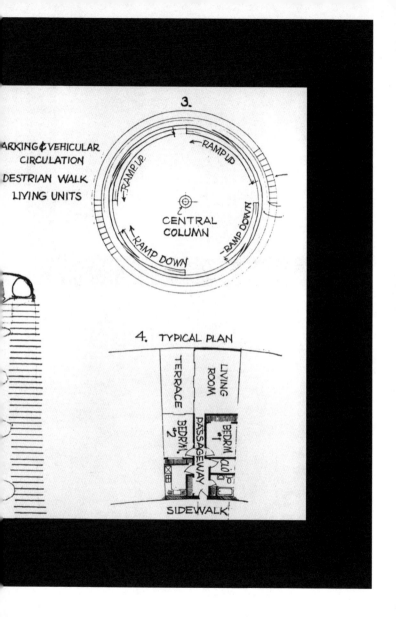

3.

PARKING & VEHICULAR
CIRCULATION

PEDESTRIAN WALK

LIVING UNITS

RAMP UP

RAMP UP

RAMP DOWN

CENTRAL
COLUMN

RAMP DOWN

RAMP DOWN

4. TYPICAL PLAN

TERRACE

LIVING
ROOM

BEDR'M.
#2

BEDR'M
#1

PASSAGEWAY

CLO

SIDEWALK

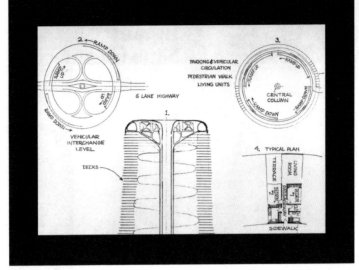

THE INCIDENTS

[*Slide*] The cylindrical towers, looking a lot like stylized nuclear cooling towers, were supposed to be flown in by helicopter and placed on top of existing housing. They would be completed while people continued to live in the houses beneath them. And once they were completed, the rest of the landscape could be razed and replaced with green space. ————"A cross section of these structures," Jordan wrote, "resembles abstract, stylized Christmas trees evenly broadening toward their base with central, supporting trunks. Each tree town is 100 circular decks high. The lowest level begins 10 stories above ground, above dust level and major cloverleaf-highway systems.Circling the central mast is a parking system of ramps that never cross. The huge interior space next permits a circling of shops, supermarkets, game rooms and workshops on every deck, plus, on some levels, a cross view of 400 feet. The penultimate circling of the central mass contains dwelling units, which provide an average of 1200 square feet"—you can see one of his units under the typical plan here, as against an average of 720 feet in today's public housing. "Every room has a view. From these hanging gardens, both rivers will be visible. "Instead of sidewalks," she wrote, "there will be wide walkways entirely separate from the cloverleaf ribbonry that will divide the high-speed through traffic from local traffic." High-speed traffic would be "separately routed over an arterial system, similar to that of the Pulaski Skyway in New Jersey. Now it becomes possible to travel from the Triborough nonstop over Manhattan Island and onto a newly created Riverspan Bridge at 125th Street into New Jersey."

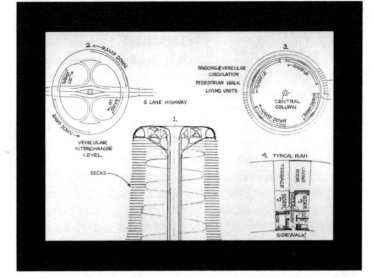

THE INCIDENTS

The article ends: "Where we are physically is enmeshed with our deepest consciousness of self. There is no evading architecture, no meaningful denial of our position. You can build to defend the endurance of man to protect his existence, to illuminate it. But you cannot build for these purposes merely in spasmodic response to past and present crises, for then crisis, like the poor, will be with us always. If man is to have not only a future but a destiny, it must be consciously and deliberately designed."——— Though Jordan and Fuller intended their project to be built, I argue that a project that is speculative and consisting of fantasy megastructures as well cannot simply be evaluated in the same way that a more traditional project might. We need the fullest aesthetic criteria to understand a project that is at once deadly serious and also exceeds the technical and urbanist criteria we have come to take for granted, and indeed the technical criteria of the time. ——— One such aesthetic tradition I would suggest is Afrofuturism. At the time, this was a kind of not-named or inchoate discourse, surfacing in the work of artists such as the musician Sun Ra who, like Buckminster Fuller, had a serious, but also fanciful, origin story: that of being born on the planet Saturn. We would have to look at these towers, then, not just as housing towers, or as cooling towers as I've suggested, but as rockets, or as boosts, as the scholar Rebecca Choi refers to them in an unpublished dissertation.

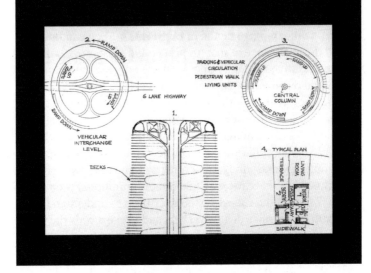

THE INCIDENTS

But it is also akin to the megastructural projects of the Metabolists, particularly with its hint of modular construction, of one tower being built on top of another. This was the period, as I've described it, of "last futures," in the words of architecture journalist Douglas Murphy, in which apocalyptic pessimism generated utopian thinking on a scale unheard of in the past. And in which "massive interior environments of the time, both imaginary and in some cases built in germinal form, were some of the purest architectural visions of social and natural harmony conceived of in human history."——— This is not treated much in urban or architectural history. But some historians who have looked at this have taken it to be a deeply anti-urban vision. The historian Daniel Matlin writes that "Skyrise" amounts to an "erasure of Harlem—the destruction or evacuation of the entire built environment within which Black Harlem's history had unfolded, and which, for all its deficiencies, had contributed powerfully to Harlem's culture, politics, and symbolic significance within African American and Black diasporic life."——— One of the most striking aspects of the proposal, indeed, is its abolition of a key locus and spatial context of so much African American sociability, expressive culture, and political mobilization: the street. But from the perspective, I argue, of how the streets were fundamentally used and dominated, Black experience—at least in Jordan's picture—was in fact excluded and often abused. Jordan and Fuller suggest an entirely different understanding that, however problematic or solipsistic on its own terms, attempts to claim free Black space that is distinct from the urban grid, which it rejects and portrays as asphyxiating.

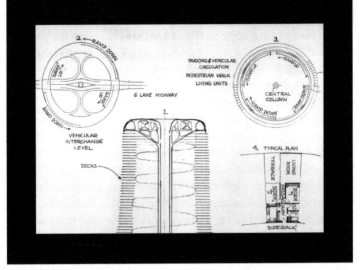

THE INCIDENTS

As Jordan wrote in her early letter to Fuller, "Given our goal of a pacific, life-expanding design for a human community, we might revise street patterning so that the present patterns of confrontation by parallel lines would never be repeated. The existing monotony limits pleasures of perspectives. Rigidly flat land is ruled by rectilinear form. The crisscrossing pattern too often becomes a psychological crucifixion; an emergence from an alleyway into a danger zone vulnerable to enemies approaching in at least two directions that converge at the target who is the pedestrian poised on a corner."

THE SKY LINE

Mother Jacobs' Home Remed

EVER since 1949, when the national Housing Act was passed, the cities of this country have been assaulted by a series of vast federally aided building operations. These large-scale operations have brought only small-scale benefits to our city. The people who gain by the government's handouts are not the displaced slum dwellers but the new investors and occupants. In the name of slum clearance, many quarters of Greater New York that would still have been decently habitable with a modest expenditure of capital have been razed, and their inhabitants, along with the shopkeepers and tavern keepers who served them, have been booted out, to resettle in even slummier quarters. Even in municipal projects designed to rehouse the displaced slum dwellers or people of equivalent low income, the physical improvements have been only partial and the social conditions of the inhabitants have been worsened through further social stratification—segregation, actual-

ly—of people b
The standard fc
by the federal gc
administrators is
structures of ten
perficially, these
immense improv
foul Old Law te
and the New L
that covered the
Bronx and the
1930. The late
only two rooms
outside exposur
widely spaced a
and patches of fc
benches. Not m
open to the sun
they are as bugpr
concrete floors a
them; they have s
water, standard
and practically e
family could den
and doors for the

THE INCIDENTS

r income levels.
housing favored
nent and big-city
rise slabs—bleak
enty stories. Su-
buildings are an
t over both the
nts of New York
901) tenements
r sections of the
West Side up to
del buildings are
all the flats have
 structures are
small play areas
rass spotted with
are the buildings
r on all sides but
d verminproof as
k walls can make
eat, hot and cold
oom equipment,
ing a well-to-do
xcept large rooms
ts; the absence of

the latter is an idiotic economy achieved at the expense of the tenants, who must provide curtains.

These buildings, with all their palpable hygienic virtues, are the response to a whole century of investigation of the conditions of housing among the lower-income groups in the big cities, particularly New York. Shortly after 1835, when the first slum tenement deliberately designed for congestion was built, on Cherry Street, the Health Commissioner of New York noted the appallingly high incidence of infant mortality and infectious diseases among the poor, and he correlated this with overcrowding of rooms, overcrowding of building plots, poor ventilation, lack of running water and indoor toilet facilities. For a large part of the nineteenth century, in all big cities, housing conditions worsened, even for the upper classes, despite the common boast that this was "the Century of Progress." It was only because of a tremendous effort by physicians, sanitarians, housing reformers, and architects that legislation established minimum standards for light, air, constructional soundness, and human decency.

Unfortunately, it turned
out that better housing was

THE SKY LINE

Mother Jacobs' Home Remedies

EVER since 1949, when the national Housing Act was passed, the cities of this country have been assaulted by a series of vast federally aided building operations. These large-scale operations have brought only small-scale benefits to our city. The people who gain by the government's handouts are not the displaced slum dwellers but the new investors and occupants. In the name of slum clearance, many quarters of Greater New York that would still have been decently habitable with a modest expenditure of capital have been razed, and their inhabitants, along with the shopkeepers and tavern keepers who served them, have been booted out, to resettle in even slummier quarters. Even in municipal projects designed to rehouse the displaced slum dwellers or people of equivalent low income, the physical improvements have been only partial and the social conditions of the inhabitants have been worsened through further social stratification—segregation, actually—of people by their income levels. The standard form of housing favored by the federal government and big-city administrators is high-rise slabs—bleak structures of ten to twenty stories. Superficially, these new buildings are an immense improvement over both the foul Old Law tenements of New York and the New Law (1901) tenements that covered the newer sections of the Bronx and the upper West Side up to 1930. The latest model buildings are only two rooms deep; all the flats have outside exposure; the structures are widely spaced around small play areas and patches of fenced grass spotted with benches. Not merely are the buildings open to the sun and air on all sides but they are as bugproof and verminproof as concrete floors and brick walls can make them; they have steam heat, hot and cold water, standard bathroom equipment, and practically everything a well-to-do family could demand except large rooms and doors for their closets; the absence of the latter is an idiotic economy achieved at the expense of the tenants, who must provide curtains.

These buildings, with all their palpable hygienic virtues, are the response to a whole century of investigation of the conditions of housing among the lower-income groups in the big cities, particularly New York. Shortly after 1835, when the first slum tenement deliberately designed for congestion was built, on Cherry Street, the Health Commissioner of New York noted the appallingly high incidence of infant mortality and infectious diseases among the poor, and he correlated this with overcrowding of rooms, overcrowding of building plots, poor ventilation, lack of running water and indoor toilet facilities. For a large part of the nineteenth century, in all big cities, housing conditions worsened, even for the upper classes, despite the common boast that this was "the Century of Progress." It was only because of a tremendous effort by physicians, sanitarians, housing reformers, and architects that legislation established minimum standards for light, air, constructional soundness, and human decency. Unfortunately, it turned out that better housing was

[*Slide*] That last quoted line has several ambiguities. On the one hand, in referring to someone who is vulnerable to enemies, it brings to mind the violence that Jordan described in the 1964 rebellion. On the other hand, it also brings forward the notion that Harlem's urban space was a zone particularly susceptible to and encouraging of crime. This is where it overlaps with the discourse of contemporary urbanism and, unusually, with another form of writing: that of Jane Jacobs. Though high-rise public housing was only a segment of all public housing worldwide, New York City has an especially high proportion of towers-in-a-park that, as we know, exude an incredible symbolic power. These towers suggest the massive scale of social investment that postwar countries poured into housing construction at the time. ——— By the 1980s, however, something resembling a nationwide consensus had been fomented against public housing for being incubators of crime and prisons of poverty. And many people blamed architects. Paul Gapp, for example, the architecture critic for *The Chicago Tribune*, wrote authoritatively, "Overall, much of the blame for the Chicago Housing Authority's failures must be attributed to architects. The influence that began with Le Corbusier has persisted, and ugly, oppressive buildings have multiplied."
——— The source of the consensus against public housing are various. In the United States, they owe in no small part to virulent racism against public housing's disproportionately African American population. But another source was a series of polemics against architecture and planning, each drawing on the other. Jane Jacobs's much admired *The Death and Life of Great American Cities* is one source of this common sense. For all of its wisdom about city planning, it is to substantial degree a book about crime prevention, which lays much, likely *too* much, at the feet of poor design. Her famous phrase, "eyes on the street," is in fact a plea for bustling street life in order to prevent crime.

THE SKY LINE

Mother Jacobs' Home Remedies

EVER since 1949, when the national Housing Act was passed, the cities of this country have been assaulted by a series of vast federally aided building operations. These large-scale operations have brought only small-scale benefits to our city. The people who gain by the government's handouts are not the displaced slum dwellers but the new investors and occupants. In the name of Greater New York that would still have been decently habitable with a modest expenditure of capital have been razed, and their inhabitants, along with the shopkeepers and tavern keepers who served them, have been booted out, to resettle in even slummier quarters. Even in municipal projects designed to rehouse the displaced slum dwellers or people of equivalent low income, the physical improvements have been only partial and the social conditions of the inhabitants have been worsened through further social stratification—segregation, actually—of people by their income levels. The standard form of housing favored by the federal government and big-city administrators is high-rise slabs—bleak structures of ten to twenty stories. Superficially, these new buildings are an immense improvement over both the foul Old Law tenements of New York and the New Law (1901) tenements that covered the newer sections of the Bronx and the upper West Side up to 1930. The latest model buildings are only two rooms deep; all the flats have outside exposure; the structures are widely spaced around small play areas and patches of fenced grass spotted with benches. Not merely are the buildings open to the sun and air on all sides but they are as bugproof and verminproof as concrete floors and brick walls can make them; they have steam heat, hot and cold water, standard bathroom equipment, and practically everything a well-to-do family could demand except large rooms and doors for their closets; the absence of the latter is an idiotic economy achieved at the expense of the tenants, who must provide curtains.

These buildings, with all their palpable hygienic virtues, are the response to a whole century of investigation of the conditions of housing among the lower-income groups in the big cities, particularly New York. Shortly after 1835, when the first slum tenement deliberately designed for congestion was built, on Cherry Street, the Health Commissioner of New York noted the appallingly high incidence of infant mortality and infectious diseases among the poor, and he correlated this with overcrowding of rooms, overcrowding of building plots, poor ventilation, lack of running water and indoor toilet facilities. For a large part of the nineteenth century, in all big cities, housing conditions worsened, even for the upper classes, despite the common boast that this was "the Century of Progress." It was only because of a tremendous effort by physicians, sanitarians, housing reformers, and architects that legislation established minimum standards for light, air, construction soundness, and human decency.

Unfortunately, it turned out that better housing was

Reviewing the book for the *New Yorker*, Lewis Mumford—in an article, shown here, that was titled, "Mother Jacobs' Home Remedies," and which is full of casual misogyny—notes this insistently, in a way that has otherwise been lost in much of the book's reception. "Underneath her thesis," he writes, "that the sidewalk, the street, and the neighborhood, in all their higgledy-piggledy unplanned casualness, are the very core of a dynamic urban life—lies a preoccupation that is almost an obsession: the prevention of criminal violence in big cities." Mumford continues, "From her point of view, one of the chief mischiefs of contemporary planning is that it reduces the number of streets by creating superblocks reserved almost exclusively for pedestrian movement, free from through wheeled traffic, with the space once preempted by unnecessary paved streets turned into open areas for play or provided with benches for the sedentary enjoyment of adults. Such a separa-tion of automobile and pedestrian runs counter to her private directives for a safe and animated neighborhood; namely, to multiply the number of cross streets, to greatly widen the sidewalks, to reduce all other open spaces, and to place many types of shops and services on streets now devoted solely to residences. This street is her patent substitute for the more diversified meeting places that traditional cities have always boasted. What is behind Mrs. Jacobs' idea of assigning exclu-sively to the street the mixed functions and varied activities of a well-balanced neighborhood unit? The answer, I repeat, is simple: Her ideal city is mainly an organization for the preven-tion of crime." He notes that Jacobs laments many of the great parks of New York City as an invitation to crime. Though Jacobs herself was insistent that design could not be the source, or the solution, for social ills—a manner of thinking she labeled "the physical fallacy"—her own conclusions were ambiguous on this front, and few of her acolytes took care to avoid environmental determinism in their own proposals.

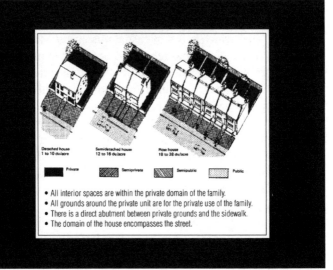

- All interior spaces are within the private domain of the family.
- All grounds around the private unit are for the private use of the family.
- There is a direct abutment between private grounds and the sidewalk.
- The domain of the house encompasses the street.

Drawing on Jacobs, the Canadian architect and planner Oscar Newman pointed to the criminogenic potential of dark stair-wells and blind corridors in Corbusier-style high-rise projects. Giving access to New York City's project, he developed an impressive taxonomy of apartment towers, and he coined the phrase "defensible space" to describe a model for residential environments that inhibits crime by creating the physical expression of a social fabric that defends itself. And you have an image here of what he had in mind. ——— And he made the case for low-rise construction in a book of the same name, *Defensible Space*. Though received consciously and ambiva-lently by his architectural peers, he was a skilled practitioner of the same urbanist invective that brought Jacobs to prom-inence. "It is inconceivable that one genius alone could have been responsible for its creation," he writes breathlessly of the public housing project. "The bare and red brick towers stand out as prominent landmarks in all our cities. Well-built monuments to a half-hearted attempt at benevolence." His book, *Defensible Space*, became the best-selling architecture book of the 1970s. His theories came to be widely adopted, and he worked as a consultant to various housing authorities in the United States. [*Slide*] It was under Newman's influence that the HOPE VI Program, initiated under President Bill Clinton, led to the demolition of high-rise public housing everywhere, and the replacement with low-rise housing, or with former res-idents being given so-called Section 8 rental vouchers to assist with finding private apartments or homes.

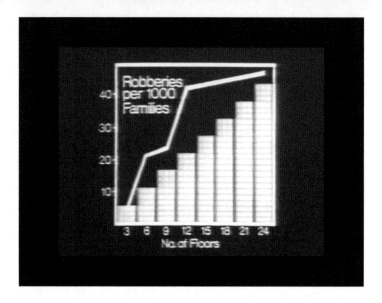

THE INCIDENTS

In David Simon's 2015 HBO miniseries, *Show Me a Hero*, based on Lisa Belkin's 1999 book about the integration of public housing in Yonkers, Oscar Newman appears with his distinctive Amish-styled beard to propagate the wisdom of low-rise, suburban-style tract homes. In the closing credits to the series, Simon indicates, "the public housing theories of Oscar Newman are now widely accepted."——— Not only were they widely accepted, they were widely traveled. [*Slide*] In the 1970s, a British researcher named Alice Coleman found *Defensible Space* in a bookstore in Canada. This discovery would change the fate of British public housing. Following Newman's lead and in consultation with him, Coleman surveyed the housing in two broad areas of London. She coined the term "problem estates" to describe poor, depressed public housing developments where she felt bad architecture had led to crime. ——— Her 1985 book, *Utopia on Trial*, is a compendium of small planning offenses: ill-lit walkways, ill-defined public and private domains, overlooked communal areas, vandalism, all delivered in a tone of utter horror. *Defensible Space* noted five or six physical characteristics that reinforced criminal behavior. *Utopia on Trial* noted 16.

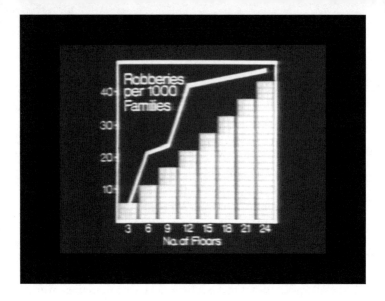

THE INCIDENTS

Coleman even brought a touch of unreconstructed Social Darwinism to her case when she argued, "The first half of the 20th century was dominated by the age-old system of natural selection, which left people free to secure the best accommodation they could." This organic system, alas, was fatefully intervened by a paternalistic authority and its utopian ideal of housing. Like *Defensible Space*, *Utopia on Trial* was criticized by peers in the field, and welcomed by political figures who saw in it a means to an end. ——— "Coleman's dismissal of the influence of poverty is based on an unsound method and an inadequate theoretical analysis," ran one contemporary review. "Her recommendations for policy are, in consequence, a diversion from the real needs and issues." Despite, and perhaps a little because of, her unsound methods, Coleman received an invitation from Prime Minister Margaret Thatcher, and she was put in charge of an experimental program to regenerate council estates on the lines of defensible space. This had enormous consequences for the global image of public housing. As historian John Boughton writes in his recent book, *Municipal Dreams: The Rise and Fall of Council Housing*, "while repair and service were things that council estates needed, it was nonetheless premised on the proposition that it is the states, and by extension the model of housing provision they represent themselves, that failed."——— This was part of a broader disinvestment from public housing. In 1980, Thatcher instituted a policy proverbially known as a "right to buy," which allowed residents of council estates to buy their apartments. At which point, the apartments then became eligible to enter the private real-estate market and ceased to be public.

THE INCIDENTS

[*Slide*] One can say that it did not fully have to be this way. Somewhere between "Skyrise for Harlem" and *Defensible Space* lies a range of Black architectures that are still being considered, or reconsidered, by historians. One which I mentioned is the unfinished project Kawaida Towers, proposed by Amiri Baraka, the poet, playwright, and organizer, who was one of the founders and theories of the Black Arts Movement that began in Harlem, as a kind of spiritual and artistic counterpart to Jordan's own work. ———— Some years later, after having failed to connect the artistic work with community life in Harlem, Baraka found himself in Newark engaged in Black nationalist organizing. Having founded the Temple of Kawaida, which stands for *tradition* and *reason* in Swahili, and then securing funding and plans to build two majority Black housing towers in the city—which was stymied by Italian-American politicians, majority-white construction unions, and police—the project was ultimately beaten back. An opportunity for Black space and Black public housing that was lost. ———— [*Slide*] A final note. I was finishing this talk on Monday evening when one of my campaign staffers called to let me know that a young Black man, Walter Wallace Jr., 27 years old, pictured here, had been shot and killed by police in West Philadelphia. My campaign staffers sent me a video that detailed the shooting, which I began to watch on my phone with hands shaking, until in the video the shots rang out, and I threw the phone across my desk, unable to move or speak for several minutes. ———— Wallace had struggled with mental health for years and had been diagnosed as bipolar. His parents called an ambulance because they believed he needed support. 911 sent the police. And when he approached the police, apparently with a knife in his hand, despite his mother crying that they should put their guns down, they shot him multiple times.

THE INCIDENTS

[*Slide*] This took place only a few blocks from the place where, in 1985, Philadelphia police had dropped a bomb on a pan-African house belonging to the group MOVE, killing an entire family, burning several blocks of West Philadelphia, and leaving hundreds homeless. As I speak, we are moving toward the second election this year in Philadelphia in which the city will be under occupation by the National Guard. ——— There are few reflections I can offer here that are adequate to this moment, except that a history that has moved away from housing toward prisons, away from utopia toward police, and away from the claiming of Black space toward gentrification, displacement, and expulsion, is in need of exorcism, trans-formation, and reparations. What new forms that will take may be up to all of us. ——— Thank you so much. Thank you for inviting me to speak.

SARAH: Thank you so much for that, sadly, very timely talk, as you draw the parallel yourself there at the end. I find it fascinating and very interesting to see your argument for high-density housing through the lens of this extraordinary story of June Jordan, who I admit I didn't know about. And I realize now partly because her story has been erased, as you indicate. ――― It leads to so many questions, and I'll start with one directed more at you, although I have several about the story itself. Your interest in and your awareness of the power of housing in creating social constructs within the city leads me to wonder about your decision to run for office at the state level—particularly because housing tends to be a policy matter at the federal level, or the municipal level. Can you talk a little bit about your clear passion for, and interest in and knowledge of, housing as an issue in the United States, and how you see it as something that can be dealt with at the state level in office?

NIKIL: I principally sought state office because there are a number of different ways that the state is a kind of mediator, I would say, between federal money, federal authority, and on-the-ground work. I'll comment on a few instances of that. On the one hand, there's zoning. I think a lot of people will know there is an ongoing conversation right now about state-level zoning and the preemption of municipal zoning. Public housing, social housing, affordable housing, or really housing of any kind is often stymied by people using existing regulations. This was actually the case for the Kawaida Towers.

———— And so, people have found that the state is, in some ways, a useful, or experimental, place to work on changing that kind of zoning in order to allow particular forms of housing to be built. We see those efforts in California—controversial efforts, to be short—and in places such as Maryland and states everywhere. In Massachusetts, actually, a bill just passed this past summer that prevents exclusionary zoning and includes housing choice provisions, called An Act Enabling Partnerships for Growth. So that is just one interest of mine.

Another interest is housing finance authorities. Federal dollars are often mediated through local state housing finance authorities. So, Pennsylvania is interesting. It has a state housing finance authority, as many places do, and it is actually the first housing authority to make passive housing—green housing, or no-carbon housing—a criterion for granting low-income housing tax credits. So, it's also a way we can expand affordable housing, affordable green housing, and sustainable housing. It's marrying our environmental initiatives with racial justice and affordable housing initiatives. ——— Then, I think the state really has the power of the purse in the sense that, hopefully, we will have stimulus money coming through again. And the state determines where that goes. Just to broaden out here, in the 2009 stimulus package we all heard about "shovel-ready projects" that were to begin construction right away. The states determine where and how that works, and how that money gets spent. So, we have state-level projects that we're really advocating for, that we're really prioritizing, and that will affect the way upcoming stimulus dollars will be spent. ——— The broad idea here is that states are experimental places. A lot of what gets done at a federal level can get done in an easier way at the state level, or in a more advanced way. They're the kind of vanguard, at least in some ways, of planning ideas and housing. I hope to do that in Pennsylvania. Not many people think of Harrisburg that way, but I hope to help change that, alongside my colleagues.

SARAH: Before we go to questions from the audience the other question I had was about the high-density housing that, essentially, you advocate through the example of June Jordan and through your critique of Jane Jacobs, which I wholly subscribe to. High-density housing is environmentally sound, and that's why you can point to Manhattan as being one of the greenest cities in the United States—because of its high density and low footprint. And yet now, with the pandemic, that's been called somewhat into question. There is a new question of whether high-density housing is unhealthy. It may be ecologically smart, but unhealthy for its inhabitants in some ways. Have you rethought your interest in high density with the onset of the pandemic?

NIKIL: Yes, it would be fatuous, I think, to say that I haven't rethought it, or that I'm dogmatically committed—that would not be a good sign. But what I understand the case to be is that it's actually the number of people within a particular space—for example, within a particular apartment—that tends to be the most important factor in propagating COVID-19, or similar viruses should there be another pandemic. I think that is one of the main issues. ——— And I think density is actually a way of relieving that kind of crowding. And there can be a too simplistic an answer to this as well, in saying that we should just build tons of housing, up and up, and zone indiscriminately—I'm not suggesting that. But I am suggesting that relieving the housing burden would be a way of ensuring that there's simply more of it, and fewer people living in shared units. ——— As someone who lived in New York City with multiple roommates and in crowded conditions, it's purely an economic necessity—you just have to live that way. There are exceptions to this. There's multi-generational housing, multi-housing. I don't want to obviate that, as that's a slightly different scenario. But that's more or less how I think how about density. And so, I think it's just essential to be building more affordable housing more densely, and for ecological reasons as well. ——— In terms of this conversation, or the premise of the question, there's a way in which this Jordan project even exceeds our use here of high density. It obviously *is* a high-density project; but it's an *extreme* high-density project. So, it's speculative—it's odd enough, and it's strange enough—to such a degree, yet at the same time it is deadly serious, and so it provokes another kind of thinking. What was the reason that people thought: we have to escape this grid, we have to escape?

And I don't think we normally consider high density housing in our current context that way. It's not meant to be an escape or a rocket ship out of here. And I think that remains this kind of residue that exceeds the bounds of our current conversation around density.

> SARAH: I think that's definitely true. There are several things there, especially the idea of offering the view to a population that typically hasn't been given the view—offering a view in Harlem, and offering it through the circular tower that gives you a full view of Manhattan, and at that point seeing both rivers. But there's also the fact that it was so open in the middle, allowing for air to circulate. It's a pretty wild idea. Obviously not super resolved, but pretty wild. ——— I have several more questions but let me get to some others from the audience.

AUDIENCE VIA SARAH: Wen Wen asks about the reconstruction of New York's Harlem, based mostly on racial unrest and crime prevention, and how you would compare that to the UK, where reconstruction involved considerations of working-class struggle. She asks whether it's a class issue more in the UK, and more of a racial issue and crime prevention in the United States and in New York.

NIKIL: It's a good question. I would personally approach it cautiously, because I know the UK situation far less well. I think that there was still—and my source here is largely Stuart Hall—a fairly heavily racialized idea. Not to the same degree as the United States, but still racialized based on the idea of rising crime. I'm thinking here of Hall's book, *Policing the Crisis*. It was a sociological study about the discourse of rising crime and how it functions. The two things are certainly bound up together because of anti–working class attitudes in the UK. But also because of the extent to which crime was still associated with people of color, with Black people from the West Indies or West Africa. That was still a fairly prominent perception of council estates. But again, I say that with some reservation, because I'm not fully sure.

AUDIENCE VIA SARAH: Then now, a pretty specific question. Daniel Clarke asks, what are your thoughts about community land trusts and housing cooperatives as a means to secure land and housing for perpetuity? In addition, what are your thoughts on the recent Philadelphia housing activists' achievement in creating a community land trust with the properties that Philadelphia's housing authority has handed over?

NIKIL: I'll describe this to give some context. It's a really extraordinary development. For several months there was an encampment on the Benjamin Franklin Parkway, which, for those people who know Philadelphia, leads right to the Philadelphia Museum of Art. It's one of Philadelphia's City Beautiful monuments, and it's in one of the wealthier, subsidized neighborhoods in terms of art subsidies. There were two protests in fact: one right on the Parkway, occupying largely a softball field, and then a second right outside the Philadelphia Housing Authority's headquarters, just a bit further north.

———— The one on the Parkway was more visible, just because it's a traffic thoroughfare. If you went to the art museum or the Barnes Foundation, you saw it. And it was extremely controversial. The residents of the neighborhood, who are in the district that I'm seeking to represent, contacted me and many people about the encampment, and they wanted to be rid of it somehow. ———— And, first, I wrote an article about this— an opinion piece with a housing advocate, or an advocate for people experiencing homelessness. Encampments of this kind have grown considerably in the United States, especially since the crisis of 2007 and 2008. There are hundreds more every year. This is a major phenomenon of our cities, and it is a direct result of the affordable housing crisis.

At the same time, it was also during a pandemic. In a way, some of the conditions of the encampment were safer than some of the shelters in the city, which are not permanent, or less permanent in certain ways than an encampment. It was expressly weighed against by the CDC that you should not clear an encampment during a pandemic. So, there was a lot of jawing back and forth. The organizers of the encampment negotiated with the city. Over time they stuck it out. A number of elected city officials, at least two, were supportive. I myself was supportive of the encampments and their goals. And they won an agreement with the City to transfer several vacant city-owned properties into a community land trust. ———— In addition, many residents were squatting in unoccupied Philadelphia Housing Authority sites. The Philadelphia Housing Authority has many different sites, scattered across the city as a way of actually getting away from the concentrated housing model. But a lot of them are unoccupied and unrepaired, so people were squatting in these homes, and they were being allowed to stay. So, just to get to the land trust side, this is unprecedented. It's truly incredible. The city negotiating with the homeless encampment protest to transfer properties into a land trust. I'm completely supportive.

I had a version of this in our campaign. We campaigned on the idea of transferring vacant properties in Philadelphia into a land trust. And a land trust, again, is a form of nonprofit housing that separates, usually, the ownership and selling of homes from the land beneath it. So it's a way of keeping them permanently affordable and collectively managed. There are many varieties, but that's a generic version. It's a great model. I think the complication with the land trust is the scaling, and I think we need one, two, three—many land trusts. And nonprofits are divergent in their governance and in how they work. Some of them can be bad; there can be a bad land trust. I think we should accept that. But I think it is good, in the sense that it is a kind of cooperative model. You can come up with limited-equity co-ops, or things like that, to build on land trusts. There are many kinds of affordable models you can use.

———— With what happened in Philadelphia, I'm immensely proud to be in a city where these organizers pulled this off, to have been modestly supportive as I could be—and to have seen this pioneered, because I want to do this in state government. We want to make it easier for this to happen. I didn't know how, and then the organizers showed us all how.

SARAH: Do you think that can ever be scaled up? Or do you think there's a sort of inherent cap to that scale?

NIKIL: One way to do it—and I've spoken with some activists in Baltimore about this—is through housing trust funds. A lot of cities have housing trust funds that devote dollars, whether through mandatory inclusionary zoning, or zoning bonuses that go to the trust fund, which they use to then build affordable housing. If you make it possible for some of that money to go to land trusts, that might be one way—or to do that through a state housing trust fund, which we have and many states have—that may be a way of trying to leverage city-state federal dollars for land trusts, as opposed to new housing construction. In places like Philly, where there's so much vacant housing and so much vacant land, it's a pretty good model. Just making that available would be the main way—somehow making sure that dollars can be spent on it. That, partly, would make it doable. How big? I don't know. I haven't figured that out.

SARAH: There's a great question from Liam Fleming, asking what recommendations you have for shifting the conversation around urban design housing and spaces away from crime prevention. I think this is really key to your talk, especially in light of a new era of unrest and civil uprisings that have already led to media hysteria.

NIKIL: Yeah, this is a great question. Let me just sit on the question.

SARAH: Particularly in the United States, and this goes back to that first question from Wen Wen—the fact that crime prevention is so tied to discussions of housing here.

NIKIL: It's a difficult question. I like to think the conversation around crime and what safety means has changed. And in speaking of Philadelphia—although this year, we should acknowledge that there's really been a high number of gun violence victims in the city—I think a shift in the conversation is also partly tied to the rather impressive work of our District Attorney Larry Krasner, who is a leading figure in the progressive prosecutor movement. And this movement recognizes that prosecutorial discretion has fueled mass incarceration. And we need to get prosecutors to start charging less and stop seeking cash bail. That has actually helped to reduce the jail population. And we have to do that on a state level.

I think people are largely supportive of that effort. We're in a moment where we need to convert the abolitionist moment and the discourse around defunding the police. This is obviously very contested—not everyone thinks we should defund the police. We do feel that resources are misspent on current forms of crime prevention. Resources are misspent on police. The feeling with Walter Wallace being killed in Philadelphia is that it's a very clear instance where an ambulance was called, but the police showed up first. He struggled with mental health. There was a clear miscarriage of justice. So, by spending on social services, and spending on housing in particular, there is an opportunity here to think about shifting priorities in our budgets. ——— It's complicated when we all face austerity budgets, as we do currently. But in a way it gets everyone to think about budgets. We all have to think about state and municipal budgets. And if people are like, we've got to make difficult cuts here, then shouldn't we be thinking about transferring resources, or making cuts to things that we feel are failing us—like forms of safety, or crime prevention that are failing us? That would be my provisional answer. I think we are able to move away from it. ——— Nonetheless the legacy of this is long-lasting. I think we haven't recovered federal dollars for public housing and for affordable housing construction. Housing authorities are continuing to build in a fairly suburbanized model, and certainly in Philadelphia that's the case. Shifting that model is a large-scale problem. It used to be the case that architects did a lot of public work, but that money has also dried up. I'm not trying to blame all architects here. It's just one of these things that as a professional body, as professionals, as associations, in every place that design students, planners, etc., have the space to do this, it's something we should be thinking about. We should be creating a vision.

SARAH: I think that one way is to combine social services and cultural and community services with housing. So, in fact, if the library had been closer to June Jordan's house, if she didn't have to catch the bus and only go there once a week, imagine what she would have written. It's incredible what she was writing with that one night a week that she could escape to the library. But if you have libraries, or other services, cultural facilities, and community facilities that are attached to housing, that's also one way of helping ameliorate the relationship between housing and crime.

NIKIL: Yes, and I forgot to mention that was one of the features of these towers: there were a lot of different cultural and retail facilities.

SARAH: You mentioned the supermarket and cultural facilities there. I wondered where they were, because it was a little hard to tell. But that definitely was part of her ambition. ——— So how is it that Fuller was so complicit in her not being part of the final article? That just strikes me as so strange that that he offered no resistance to the fact that she was so written out of the final piece, when she was the one who had been approached by *Esquire* in the first place.

NIKIL: I've done a little bit of digging into Fuller's archives. I can't quite figure out—I'm hesitant to say fully yet that that was what happened, that Fuller was complicit, although it's perfectly likely. Jordan blames the *Esquire* editors themselves. And not to get too deep into Fuller, but knowing his manner of working, it just was one of many different projects that he was working on. I think they submitted a project together. And then also knowing how magazines work—that editors could come up with a title, send the proof, and it just sort of shows up. And you're like, "Uh oh, this is what happened?" I think it's a totally plausible explanation. At the same time, it's also plausible that Fuller did not resist, or had some hand in this, and then it just showed up as entirely his work. I did not even mention Shoji Sadao, the draftsman who worked closely with Fuller.

SARAH: A question about Jane Jacobs, from someone who was just at the online unveiling of a marker at her house at 555 Hudson in New York, the famous address where she wrote *Death and Life*. James is asking if you can expand on what you mean by density, and how it compares with her understanding of density. ——— A second part of his question points out how her anti-professional expertise favors listening to people who live in communities and neighborhoods, and asks whether you too listen to people. And I would argue that June Jordan also is talking to people in neighborhoods and developing a different form of expertise. But I think he wants a comparison between your reading of density and your version of listening to people in the community, compared to Jacobs.

NIKIL: I don't want to say that I'm averse to Jacobs's version of density, exactly. What I would describe it as is a kind of archetypal streetscape, which actually is quite common—there's Greenwich Village, but it's very common in Philadelphia. And it is often perfectly dense: it rivals New York City in certain cases, and it's just in many wide swaths, and it can be very useful in terms of retrofits and green housing. It can be sustainable. So, I don't want to say too much against it. ———— I think Mumford's idea of cities, which is not necessarily mine, is just that there could be a variety of different kinds of spaces. Jacobs actually accommodated street traffic, like cars, as well as sidewalks, and things like that. But he was like, well actually this obliterates so many different things that we've done in cities. Not all of which are bad. Some of which he agreed, are bad, and I think Mumford is actually much more averse some of these things, and somewhat just as averse to skyscrapers ———— What was the second part of the question?

SARAH: Relationship to the community, and listening to those who lived there.

NIKIL: Yeah, there's something I didn't get into. There's a coterminous project, or maybe it's concurrent from the late '60s, by a more architecture-focused group. J. Max Bond Jr., a Black architect, was part of this group called ARCH. They had a much more preservation-minded and street-corner focus on Harlem. I think it's more akin to Jacobs's view of things at the same time. I hesitate to repeat it because it feels like a hackneyed criticism of Jacobs, even though it's not wrong. It's just sort of resulted in preserving in amber some of the kind of ideas, like streetscapes, that depressed variety and depressed the possibility of building, of having new residents, and actually accommodating existing residents. ——— But that resulted exactly from this kind of community input and community-led process. I think we're in a funny place when it comes to planning, where—many people recognize this, and I feel this very much as an elected official, or soon-to-be-elected official—you seek to listen, and you seek community input. But then who ends up being "the community" in any given instance is a very fraught question. It can be a neighborhood association that has people pay dues and it barely represents the neighborhood. And they'll say, "Yeah, we had community input."

I think in a way we're at a point where we miss technocracy, and we miss master-planning. And there's this exhausting way in which project by project gets debated—house by house, in certain areas. And we're not able to move ambitiously or regionally. ———— That's led to rethinking how we listen to community input. It doesn't mean you don't do it. It's just thinking about what it means, and who is involved in it. I think this is what a lot of people probably feel now—planners, architects, and elected officials.

> SARAH: That would make a very good article, I think, in terms of actually tying politics to the city— in terms of understanding how we get the input of a democracy without either being flooded by social media and constructed input, or acknowledging the challenges, as you point out, to how communities are sometimes conscripted or controlled. I think it's super interesting.

But I think you do actually first have the project. And all of this is before you get elected on Tuesday, so you have a lot of writing to do between now and Tuesday. You should pitch a story on this piece, then take this piece and pitch it as a story to *Esquire*. So, I expect to see that article, as well as an article on community input and the challenges of defining community in today's democracy for advancing democratic voice at the community level. ——— I look forward to reading more of your writing. And I look forward to your success on Tuesday. Thanks so much for giving us your time, for sharing this story with us, and provoking our interest. I really appreciate it.

NIKIL: Thank you so much.

Images

P. 14 (top)   LBJ Library photo by Cecil Stoughton.

P. 14 (bottom), 16   From The New York Times. © 1964
                     The New York Times Company.
                     All rights reserved. Used under license.

P. 18   Library of Congress Prints and
                     Photographs Division.

PP. 20, 24   © Louise Bernikow.

P. 22   Nonpareil photos, "Barry & Ike,"
                     Council Bluffs Public Library,
                     https://www.councilbluffslibrary.org
                     /archive/items/show/6895.

P. 26 (top)   Associated Press.

P. 26 (bottom)   Photo by Stanley Wolfson, New York
                     World-Telegram and the Sun Newspaper
                     Photograph Collection (Library of
                     Congress).

P. 28   Photo by Dick DeMarsico, New York
                     World-Telegram and the Sun Newspaper
                     Photograph Collection (Library of
                     Congress).

SENATOR NIKIL SAVAL is a father, husband, writer, and organizer. He's proud to be raising his sons, Ishaan and Mayukh, in South Philadelphia with his wife, Shannon Garrison, a historic preservationist. Saval's organizing is deeply rooted in the labor movement. From 2009 to 2013, he was a volunteer labor organizer with UNITE HERE, organizing boycotts against luxury hotel developers to fight for the rights of housekeepers and helping to win back the jobs of noontime aides laid off because of Governor Tom Corbett's budget cuts. Saval also has extensive experience in community and electoral organizing. In 2016, he was a leader in US Senator Bernie Sanders's presidential campaign. From this experience, Saval went on to co-found Reclaim Philadelphia, a progressive organization working for racial, gender, and economic justice throughout the Philadelphia area. In 2018, he organized campaigns to fight for change in the Democratic Party and was elected as Leader of Philadelphia's Democratic Second Ward. Saval was the first Asian American to hold the position of Ward Leader in Philadelphia.

In his career as a writer, Saval has been a frequent contributor to *The New York Times* and a contributing writer for *The New Yorker*, covering architecture, design, and housing. Saval previously served as co-editor of the literary journal *n+1* and still serves on its board of directors. In 2014, Saval published his book *Cubed: A Secret History of the Workplace*. In *Cubed*, he examined the long-term evolution of the office from its roots in nineteenth-century counting houses all the way to the cubicle, ultimately presenting a world in which workplaces, and the lives of the workers within them, could be improved in the future.

SARAH M. WHITING joined the Harvard GSD as dean and Josep Lluís Sert Professor of Architecture in July 2019. She is a design principal and cofounder of WW Architecture, and served as the dean of the Rice University School of Architecture from 2010 to 2019.

Whiting has taught at Princeton University, the University of Kentucky, the Illinois Institute of Technology, and the University of Florida, in addition to Rice and the Harvard GSD. She frequently lectures throughout the United States and abroad, and regularly serves as a critic of architecture and urban design. Prior to founding WW, Whiting worked with the Office for Metropolitan Architecture in Rotterdam; Peter Eisenman in New York; and Michael Graves in Princeton, New Jersey. She is an associate member of the American Institute of Architects.

Whiting's research is broadly interdisciplinary, with the built environment at its core. An expert in architectural theory and urbanism, she has particular interests in architecture's relationship with politics, economics, and society and how the built environment shapes the nature of public life. Her work has been published in leading journals and collections, and she is the founding editor of Point, a book series aimed at shaping contemporary discussions in architecture and urbanism.